Original title:
The Secret to Life (It's Not Really a Secret)

Copyright © 2025 Creative Arts Management OÜ
All rights reserved.

Author: Juliette Kensington
ISBN HARDBACK: 978-1-80566-164-1
ISBN PAPERBACK: 978-1-80566-459-8

The Beauty of Imperfection

A crooked smile, a missing shoe,
The world is messy, that much is true.
With every flaw, a tale unfolds,
In every crack, a treasure holds.

Embrace the chaos, let laughter ring,
For life's oddities are quite the swing.
A broken vase, a laugh or two,
In the jumbled puzzle, find joy anew.

In the Cracks of Routine

Coffee spills and pants that tear,
Morning routines lead us anywhere.
A missed bus ride, a tripped up toe,
In these moments, let your laughter flow.

Stuck in traffic, a funny tune,
This mundane rhythm makes us swoon.
For in the monotony, surprises burst,
It's life's little quirks that quench our thirst.

Forgotten Keys to Happiness

Lost my keys, oh what a plight,
Found them in the fridge, what a sight!
Happiness hid in silly things,
Like dancing with cats while the doorbell rings.

A grocery list that takes a twist,
Buying donuts when you meant to risk.
In every misstep, a giggle waits,
Life's laughter blooms behind closed gates.

The Treasure in Mundane Moments

Dust bunnies dancing, oh what a show,
Washing socks, a comedy flow.
Chasing children or running late,
These tiny dramas, oh aren't they great?

A missed appointment, a cat that steals,
The little antics double our thrills.
In the ordinary, joy does bloom,
Finding gold in every cluttered room.

Embracing the Marvel of Now

The clock ticks, yet we dance,
With mismatched socks, we prance.
Life's a stage, and we're the jest,
Skipping chores, we do our best.

Each coffee sip holds a tale,
With giggles that will never pale.
Tomorrow's worries are just fluff,
Right now's the moment, and it's enough.

Threads of Connection

Weaving laughter through our day,
Like cats on strings, we sway.
With silly hats and wiggly moves,
Our hearts beat loud, and laughter grooves.

A text, a meme, a call just for fun,
Keeping friendships bright, second to none.
In this tangled web we create,
We've found the glue while we await.

When Tomorrow Meets Today

Tomorrow's plans may go astray,
But who can care? Let's laugh and play!
With cookies burnt and dishes piled,
A giggle here makes chaos mild.

In the midst of messy bliss,
We find our joy in moments amiss.
Let's dance between the here and now,
Forget the frowns and take a bow!

The Uncharted Landscape of Living

Adventures await on this wild ride,
With rubber ducks and a playful slide.
Maps are nice, but so is chance,
Let's twirl in circles, join the dance.

With hiccups and leaps, we draw our way,
In laughter's light, we boldly sway.
Every misstep is a step divine,
Life's goofy script is truly fine.

The Moments Between Moments

In the pause of a hiccup,
Life does its little dance.
A cat on a windowsill,
Watching life happen by chance.

A squirrel with a nut,
Daring fate with a leap.
Each giggle we hold close,
Is a memory we keep.

So here's to the snickers,
And the giggles that come fast.
In the quiet of chaos,
These moments are meant to last.

With each tick of the clock,
Let's treasure the wink and nod.
For in between the big things,
Is where we find the odd.

Capturing Fleeting Glances

A smile from a stranger,
Like sunshine on a rainy day.
We share a knowing look,
In an odd, delightful way.

The wink of an eyelash,
The nod of a friend.
These tiny little moments,
Are what we recommend.

A brief touch on the shoulder,
A laugh that bursts like fizz,
In a world full of rush,
Look close—find the bliss!

So snap those quick seconds,
Before they melt away.
Life's giggles are slippery,
Catch them before they sway.

Silent Reflections by the River

Sitting by the water,
Where ripples take their turns.
A frog jumps with a plop,
As the sun slowly burns.

Leaves whisper their gossip,
The pebbles play hide and seek.
Nature's own comedy,
In the silence, we peek.

A duck quacks a joke,
At the fish swimming low.
Every splash is a giggle,
In a big, watery show.

So breathe in the stillness,
Let laughter float free.
For in the rivers of laughter,
Life's punchlines find glee.

The Wisdom of Ancient Echoes

Ancient trees have seen it all,
From secrets to silly tunes.
Their branches sway and whisper,
'Don't take life too seriously, you goons!'

Echoes of laughter linger,
In the hollows of the wood.
Every chuckle they remember,
Is a moment truly good.

So let's lean on the bark,
And talk to the wise old oak.
In the shadow of wisdom,
Life becomes a grand joke.

With each rustle and creak,
Their tales flutter and glide.
If trees can keep laughing,
So should we—right by their side!

The Unseen Symphony of Existence

In a world where squirrels plot,
Their acorn heists, oh what a plot.
We laugh at cats, they rule the street,
With glorious twirls, a tiny feat.

Life's rhythm skips, just like a stone,
Caffeine buzz, never alone.
A dance of socks, mismatched dare,
Find joy in chaos; we all share.

Each sandwich made with flair and might,
Peanut butter spread just right.
Time winks at us from the clock,
Laugh with a grin and then just rock!

Bubbles float, then meet the floor,
Fizzy giggles, what's in store?
Unseen music plays all around,
Join the merry jigs we found.

A Mosaic of Moments Yet to Come

Jellybeans in a jar so bright,
Choose your color, what a sight!
Life's a puzzle, bits and pieces,
Each laugh shared, the joy increases.

In the kitchen, flour flies high,
A cake unfolds, a sweet goodbye.
Life's adventures, so absurd,
Finding meaning in a bird.

A wild dream rides a bicycle,
Wobbly wheels, so comical.
Chasing sunsets in paper boats,
Adventures await, with silly notes.

The future's bright, a kaleidoscope,
Twists and turns, with a hint of hope.
Let's dance through hours, sip some tea,
In this grand joke, just you and me.

The Unnoticed Dance of Life

Underneath the starlit sky,
Fireflies blink, they wave bye-bye.
A rabbit hops in mismatched shoes,
Life twirls on, but we rarely snooze.

Silly hats on our heads so proud,
Jumping puddles in a joyful crowd.
Every hiccup, every blunder,
Turns our frowns into pure thunder.

Doodle monsters dance in dreams,
Waving arms, or so it seems.
Flip-flops squeak on the beach parade,
Life's funny moments never fade.

Tickling toes in the grass so green,
We find the bliss in the unseen.
So let's skip through this curious land,
With laughter and joy, hand in hand.

Where Dreams Breathe

In a cupboard full of yearning dreams,
Here lies laughter, or so it seems.
A pillow fight, a giggle spree,
Where day meets night, let spirits free.

Clouds of fluff and candy skies,
Dreams whispering silly goodbyes.
Each chuckle paints the canvas bright,
Twirling tales in the moonlight.

A purple cat on a skateboard flies,
Chasing butterflies through azure skies.
Life's a game of hop and skip,
With every sip, let laughter drip.

Chasing rainbows with goofy hats,
Finding humor, where laughter's at.
For every twirl, the heart beats fast,
In this funny dance, forever cast.

The Forgotten Language of the Heart

When hearts do talk in silence,
They send a wink, not violence.
A glance, a nod, a little grin,
Is where the tales of love begin.

A smirk can light a gloomy day,
While giggles chase the clouds away.
Forget the rules, just let it flow,
Let laughter teach what hearts should know.

In every smile, a world unfolds,
With jokes and puns, the truth it holds.
So tune your ears to what's unsaid,
And paint your life in joy instead.

For language switches with a sigh,
And speaks in means that can't deny.
When hearts connect in silly ways,
Life's merry dance forever plays.

A Mosaic of Fleeting Moments

Life's a puzzle made of laughs,
With missing pieces, quirky drafts.
A tickle here, a playful poke,
In every moment, joy's the joke.

The mundane sparkles with delight,
Like socks that vanish out of sight.
A bumblebee in search of cake,
Transforms the day we thought was fake.

Each tiny blip, a gem we find,
Like mismatched shoes that fate combined.
So gather up each silly scene,
And stitch a quilt of in-between.

For laughter's glue, it binds us tight,
In fleeting moments, pure and bright.
Collect the quirks, and frame them high,
In life's mad tapestry, we fly.

Navigating the Currents of Existence

Life's a river, wide and strange,
With gummy bears that bounce and change.
We float along on lopsided ducks,
Embracing all the awkward plucks.

Bumping boats and silly rows,
In waters blue, where laughter flows.
An oar that's bent, a snagged old hat,
Each twist and turn is where it's at.

With whirlpools made of jelly beans,
And mermaids sporting wobbly jeans.
We paddle past the norm with cheer,
And laugh at what we hold so dear.

In waves of whimsy, we are tossed,
Each splash a lesson, never lost.
Grab a snack, let go the strife,
For joy's the map that guides our life.

Chasing Rainbows in the Mist

In stormy skies, we find the fun,
With rubber boots, we leap and run.
Each droplet spins a crazy tale,
As we become the stormy gale.

Chasing colors through the haze,
We'll paint the world in laughter's blaze.
A giggle here, a splatter there,
No need for reason, just a dare.

With kites of dreams, we dance and soar,
Forget the downpour; it's just decor.
We splash in puddles, laugh and shout,
As rainbows form where doubts cast out.

So find the joy in every drop,
Where smiles bloom and worries stop.
For in the mist, we leave our mark,
Chasing crayon rainbows, wild and stark.

Echoes of Everyday Wisdom

If socks go missing, don't fret the loss,
Just embrace the chaos, it's worth the toss.
Spilt milk's not tragic, just cereal's fate,
Laugh it away, don't let worries wait.

Lemons on your counter can't start a fight,
Add some sugar, turn wrongs to right.
Life's best advice? Just eat dessert first,
Frolic in sweetness, quench the thirst.

When traffic's a nightmare, just sing a tune,
Join the car chorus, your own little boon.
Life's a wild ride, sometimes you swerve,
With laughter and joy, that's how you serve.

So here's to the missteps, the trips, and the falls,
For every small stumble, your spirit enthralls.
Dance in the rain, let giggles ignite,
For fun sprinkled freely makes everything bright.

Hidden Treasures of the Heart

Underneath your bed, dust bunnies unite,
They're treasures of laughter, a comical sight.
Find joy in the crevices, giggles unfold,
In every lost shoe, a story retold.

Cats in the window, plotting their schemes,
Chasing the sunlight, living their dreams.
Each purr is a whisper, wisdom so sly,
The best kind of lesson? Just give it a try.

A half-eaten sandwich, old popcorn remains,
Signal to me that joy sometimes wanes.
Yet laughter's the prize that never grows old,
When sharing your lunches, let stories be told.

So keep your heart light and your treasure near,
In every small moment, let mirth appear.
For life's a buffet, not just a plain meal,
Savor the bites, let your laughter reveal.

A Map of Invisible Journeys

Draw maps in the sand with fingers and toes,
The ocean might wash them, but laughter still grows.
Each wave a reminder of fun far and wide,
Adventure's a journey, not always a ride.

Wander through life with a whimsical eye,
In puddles and shadows, let bright spirits fly.
Pretend you're an explorer of uncharted lands,
Sometimes a detour makes the best plans.

Invisible journeys can lead you afar,
With friends as your compass, you shine like a star.
Each giggle a milestone, map points of joy,
So dress like a pirate, be brave, and enjoy!

Collect all your treasures, both silly and bold,
In stories and laughter, you'll never grow old.
For life's a grand voyage filled with delight,
Set sail on the giggles, embrace the night.

Lessons Beneath the Stars

Under a blanket of twinkling display,
Count how many wishes slip into the fray.
Stars can't tell secrets from far in the sky,
But laughter's the currency, so give it a try.

A comet's just a rock on a high-speed spree,
But imagine its tales; oh, where could it be?
Traveling through cosmos, lost and adrift,
It whispers to dreamers, "Let laughter be gift."

The moon chuckles softly, a glow on our face,
As we dance in the night, cherishing our place.
Sirens of starlight will sing from afar,
Life's lessons are simple: just be who you are.

So marvel at wonders, shine bright and be bold,
Crack jokes with the universe, let stories unfold.
In the dance of the night, find the joy that astounds,
For laughter's the magic where true love abounds.

Beneath the Stars We Wander

Under a sky so wide and bright,
We ask if aliens might share a bite.
With burgers flying through the air,
We laugh and wonder, do they care?

A UFO lands for a quick snack,
Out pops a chef, no beef to lacking.
"Take me to your leader," we jest,
Only to offer him a slice of zest.

Moons of cheese and planets of pie,
We spin in circles, oh my, oh my!
Gravity's a friend when we're so light,
Dance beneath the stars all night.

Lessons from the Gentle Breeze

The breeze tiptoes with a playful sway,
Whispering secrets of the day.
"Hold your hat tight," it warns with glee,
As it lifts the mailman up a tree.

It flirts with flowers and teases the trees,
"Catch me if you can!" it calls to bees.
Global warming, it rolls its eyes,
And blows a cool kiss that's oh so wise.

From the playground swings, laughter takes flight,
The breeze rolls in, making it right.
It teaches us how to just let be,
Life's more fun when you float like a leaf.

The Language of Shared Smiles

Two strangers meet, the sparkling light,
A smile exchanged, oh what a sight!
No need for words, noplex to decode,
Just a grin as we stroll down the road.

A child drops ice cream, and soon we laugh,
With sticky fingers, we share the gaffe.
The baker who winks while icing his buns,
Unites us all, with warmth and fun.

In crowded trains, with faces so grim,
One subtle grin brings joy on a whim.
This bond we share, so sweet and true,
Is the glue that holds us as we pass through.

Unfolding in Unexpected Places

A paper crane flutters in the wind,
In a coffee shop, where dreams begin.
"Just fold it right, and you will see,"
Sips of laughter with that cup of tea.

Found an old sock in a fancy shoe,
Wondered if it belonged to you.
With laughter and chaos, the scene unfolds,
The warmth of friendship in moments untold.

The cat who wears glasses, what a sight!
Sipping milk, zen and white.
Life's little quirks remind us each day,
Are the colorful strokes of a whimsical play.

Nature's Quiet Counsel

Birds sing sweetly in the trees,
Squirrels chase with silly ease.
Life's a giggle, don't you see?
Let's laugh more, you and me!

Clouds dance gently in the sky,
A playful breeze floats by.
Nature whispers funny ways,
To brighten up our days.

Catch a leaf that swirls around,
Watch it tumble to the ground.
In each moment, find your cheer,
Nature's humor is right here!

So don't fret or wear a frown,
Life can turn your mood around.
Let joy bloom like flowers bright,
It's a joke, but feels just right!

Finding Gold in Mundane Moments

Chores can spark a giggle spree,
Dust bunnies dance, so carefree!
Finding treasure in the mess,
A laugh could be the best success!

Laundry piles, a mountain high,
But socks in pairs, oh me, oh my!
Each cycle spins a tale so grand,
Who knew laundry could be so planned?

Coffee spills on worn-out jeans,
A fashion choice from silly scenes.
Small victories, we must embrace,
In every laugh, find your place!

Even in traffic, time to unwind,
Fantastic tunes, the peace you'll find.
When life feels dull, just look around,
In the mundane, joy is found!

The Magic of Now

Each tick and tock, a chance for fun,
Dance like you're the only one.
The moment sparkles, bright and new,
In today's magic, just be you!

Forget tomorrow, it's a haze,
Join the silly, sing your praise.
Time's a jester, quirky and wild,
Embrace the laughter like a child!

Coffee's hot, savor the taste,
Muffin crumbs, no need for haste.
Life's a party, don't you know?
In every breath, let chuckles flow!

So grab your moment, hold it tight,
Joke and laugh, it feels just right.
In this magic, find your glow,
Here's your ticket, enjoy the show!

Invisible Connections of Being

We are threads in a big old quilt,
Woven tight, with jokes to be built.
With a nod and a wink we share,
Invisible ties float in the air!

A smile from a stranger's face,
Turns the day into a happier place.
In the laughter, we connect,
In this web, we all reflect!

Let's pretend we're fish in streams,
Swimming along with goofy dreams.
Each splash and giggle, a link so bright,
In unity, we find delight!

So reach for joy, hold on tight,
Every chuckle feels just right.
These ties may seem like silly things,
But oh, the magic that laughter brings!

A Dance of Unseen Forces

In the kitchen, pots collide,
The cat guides the spoons like a tide.
Spaghetti flies with a twirl and a spin,
While laughter erupts from within.

Life's a tango, a jolly parade,
With mismatched socks, join the charade.
We stumble and trip, but who needs finesse?
It's all about smiles, I must confess.

Invisible threads bind each wild move,
Like a game that fate aims to prove.
The dance of the clumsy, the wacky embrace,
We swirl through our tasks with sheer silly grace.

So grab a broom, take a turn with bring,
Make the mundane feel like a fling.
For the cheer of each moment, we pirouette in glee,
In this quirky festival, just you and me.

Sunlight Through the Cracks

Cracks in the walls let the sunshine peek,
While dust bunnies gather, and old chairs squeak.
The coffee spills over, a caffeinated mess,
But we laugh harder, I must confess.

The floorboards creak like they're singing a song,
As mismatched socks dance where they don't belong.
We toast our day with cereal and cheer,
For the warm glow of morning is always near.

Sunlight filters through with a golden hue,
Timing's a joke, as it slips from view.
Every bright moment, a sweet little prank,
Life's a laugh track, in a glorious flank.

So here's to the beams that slap through the gaps,
Reminding us all, it's fun that unwraps.
Let's crack open laughter, a dazzling ray,
In this goofball melody, we find our way.

The Joy in Ordinary Days

Waking up to socks on the floor,
A melody plays from the fridge's door.
Coffee brews loudly, a raucous parade,
On ordinary days, merriment's made.

The toaster pops like it's out for a dance,
As toast flies high, giving breakfast a chance.
A sprinkle of chaos, a dash of delight,
In the rhythm of mornings, we'll take flight.

Sidewalks become runways for brunch,
With strangers that wave as they munch.
The simple absurdities come out to play,
In the joyous confetti of an average day.

So here's to the giggles in traffic's slow crawl,
And moments of magic that spark from it all.
For the world keeps on spinning, cheeky and spry,
In these unremarkable days, we laugh 'til we cry.

Tapestry of Unspoken Wisdom

Threads of laughter weave in my mind,
In moments of silence, insights unwind.
Like the dog that barks at shadows and light,
We chase echoes of wisdom, day and night.

Unraveled truths hide in simple play,
A joke on the tongue that just won't stay.
The way the cat rules each couch and rest,
Sends a message we often forget to contest.

In the fabric of life, stitches fray and bend,
Yet, hilarity patches where we might offend.
So let's toast to the mess of all we create,
In this quirky tapestry, we celebrate fate.

With threads of humor we boldly sew,
Crafting a quilt from the tales of our woe.
For within every giggle lies a great piece of lore,
In our tapestry woven, we always want more.

Whispers of the Heart

In a world of plans so grand,
We find joy in grains of sand.
Laughter bubbles, tickles your soul,
Life's just a game, let's take a stroll.

With a wink and a silly grin,
We dance like no one's watching in.
Forget the map, embrace the chance,
You might just stumble, lose your pants!

Every hiccup, every fall,
Is just a giggle, a fun call.
So swing your arms, let loose your hair,
Life's a circus, come join the fair!

So lift your cup, toast to the day,
In the silliest, most glorious way.
With every moment, twirl and spin,
In this game, my friend, we always win!

Hidden Threads of Existence

Life's a puzzle, pieces askew,
Sometimes we stumble, that's nothing new.
Chasing rainbows, tripping on stairs,
Finding fortune in worn-out chairs.

In every corner, a mystery lurks,
Like socks that vanish; oh, how it irks!
But giggles echo through the strife,
Woven joy, the fabric of life.

Sprinkle laughter, like confetti in air,
Dance in the shower, shake off despair.
With every moment, stitch a thread,
Watch the tapestry swirl in your head.

So toast to chaos, embrace the mess,
In the weirdness, we find our best.
Life's quirks are treasures, don't you see?
In the whirl, that's where we're free!

Unraveled Mysteries of Being

Why do we worry, oh what a plight?
The cat's on the roof, such a silly sight.
Chasing our tails, like a dog with treats,
Pretending we know where the real fun meets.

With every error, a lesson learned,
Like burning the toast that we once yearned.
Life's a sitcom, let's crack a smile,
Even the mishaps have a certain style.

So sing out loud, let the neighbors hear,
Life's just a riddle, we'll persevere.
Paint your day, with colors bold,
Each silly moment, a joy to unfold.

At the end of our quest, we'll just say,
"Who knew it was fun in such a way?"
Let's lift our glasses, embrace the fun,
In this crazy life, we've already won!

Echoes in Everyday Moments

In mornings bright, a toast we raise,
To spilled coffee and endless maze.
The dog steals socks, a cat's sly pounce,
Chasing our woes, we laugh and bounce.

Every stumble, a dance we do,
With mischief painted in shades of blue.
Each crazy moment, a melody sweet,
In the symphony, let's tap our feet!

So wear your quirks, like a badge of pride,
Join the parade, there's nothing to hide.
With every chuckle, we weave our thread,
In this joyous tapestry, we're gently led.

As the sun dips low, let's share a grin,
For the grandest journey is where we've been.
With every echo, let laughter ring,
In the mundane, we find our zing!

The Canvas of Now

Every moment's a brush stroke,
Splashing colors on the page.
Don't forget to laugh, my friend,
It's the best paint for any age.

Messy lines create the fun,
Shapes and shades that intertwine.
Who needs perfection, anyway?
Keep it silly, drink some wine!

Life's a canvas, wild and bright,
Throw confetti in the air.
A happy accident feels right,
Let out giggles everywhere!

So dance and twirl, embrace the fun,
Leave behind your heavy load.
In the art of now, we run,
On a rainbow, we're all strode.

The Art of Appreciating Whispers

In a world so loud and bright,
Listen close, there's joy in whispers.
Tiny secrets take their flight,
Check for giggles, they're good sisters.

A breeze might carry sighs so sweet,
Like candy gifts that float on by.
Eavesdrop on a busy street,
You'll find laughter in the sigh.

Watch for grins in quiet nooks,
Between the chatter, hearts collide.
In gentle jokes and playful looks,
The essence of glee can't hide!

So tune your ears to whispered cheer,
Catch the chuckles in the air.
With each soft sound that you hear,
Life's lightest moments, we all share.

Finding Light in the Shadows

In every shadow, light does creep,
Underneath that dark facade.
Search for giggles, not just sleep,
Lurking near that leafy plod.

Playful shadows dance around,
Making shapes that bend and twist.
In the silence, joy is found,
Amidst the fog, don't be missed!

A shadow's just a friend in gloom,
Whispers low and gently cheer.
Turn your frown into a bloom,
Sprinkle fun on every fear!

When life dims, you'll find a spark,
Hidden in the playful throng.
So let the shadows make their mark,
And join the chorus of the strong.

Embracing Uncertainty's Embrace

Oh, uncertainty, you quirky mate,
You shake the ground beneath my feet.
With you, the plans are just a bait,
But oh, you make life such a treat!

Like a piñata, we take swings,
Expecting sweets, but getting dust.
That's the fun; it's what life brings,
In crazy twists, we learn to trust.

So what if plans go off the rail?
The surprises bring a laugh so bright.
Embrace the ride, you cannot fail,
In chaos, find your heart's delight!

So hold my hand, let's leap and bound,
Dance in the face of all unknowns.
In every spin, joy will be found,
As we juggle life's funny tones.

The Elegance of Every Breath

Inhale the laughter on a sunny day,
Exhale the worries, watch them sway.
Life's a dance, a silly jig,
Waltzing through troubles, feeling big.

Sipping on dreams like sweet lemonade,
Fumbling through moments, never afraid.
Twirling in socks on a polished floor,
Finding the joy in the mundane chore.

Painting with Colors of Experience

Brush strokes of blunders paint the best,
Each splash of color brings a jest.
With a palette of smiles and goofy grins,
We mix up the trouble, that's where it begins.

Life's a canvas, get a bit splashed,
A masterpiece born from each moment crashed.
Doodles of laughter in every hue,
Creating a picture that feels so true.

The Unseen Patterns of Joy

Like socks that vanish in a dryer spin,
Joy leaps out, a whimsical grin.
In the chaos of canines chasing tails,
We find the treasure, where laughter prevails.

Patterns emerge in a pie made of glee,
Serendipity winked and said, "Look at me!"
A jigsaw puzzle with pieces that play,
Helping us navigate the silliest way.

Little Secrets of the Heart

Whispers of giggles tucked in the air,
Winks from the universe, tiny and rare.
Hiccups of joy in unexpected places,
Dancing through life with silly faces.

The heart knows secrets, a wink and a nudge,
It laughs at the weight that we refuse to budge.
Unraveling mysteries with a chuckle and cheer,
Finding pure bliss as we joke without fear.

The Hidden in Plain Sight

In a sock drawer, wisdom hides,
Among the lint, where knowledge bides.
Your lost keys dance with every thought,
Unlocking dreams that time forgot.

The cat knows more than we will share,
With knowing glances, a royal stare.
Her majesty rules the sunbeam's throne,
While we chase shadows, yet feel alone.

Revelations in the Rearview Mirror

Last week's lunch stick to my thighs,
My car sees all, much to my surprise.
Who knew my flaws could come alive,
In the tinted glass, I can't disguise?

The fast-food wrappers, they tell a tale,
Of fries with dreams that sometimes fail.
A messy backseat, like life's own floor,
Is where I find treasures I adore.

The Heartbeat of Everyday

Coffee spills echo morning sighs,
A dance of chaos under clear blue skies.
The toast insists on being burnt,
Yet it's the little things that truly turn.

At stoplights, we form a band on wheels,
Miming solos, sharing our feels.
Each honk a chord, each glance a note,
In this crazy symphony, we all float.

Echoes of Laughter and Tears

The fridge hums tunes of midnight snacks,
While laughter spills from old, worn tracks.
We cry at movies, yet laugh at our fate,
Finding comfort in pies we create.

A soggy tissue, our badge of pride,
In the messy moments, joy can't hide.
So let's toast to life, with coffee or cheer,
For every hiccup brings us near.

Chasing Shadows of Forgotten Dreams

I chased a shadow down the street,
It winked at me with sneaky feet.
I offered it a cup of tea,
It laughed and danced, said 'Not for me.'

In search of dreams that slipped away,
Like socks that vanish in the fray.
I found a pair beneath the bed,
But they were not the dreams I bred.

With every hiccup, every sigh,
I stumble forth and wonder why.
But with a giggle, I press on,
For what is lost can still be fun!

So here I am, no map in hand,
Just stumbling through this wonderland.
With shadows flickering along my path,
I laugh out loud and embrace the math.

A Whisper from Forgotten Passages

In old, creaky halls, I heard a sound,
A whisper that spun my head around.
It told me jokes from days of yore,
And I giggled until my sides were sore.

The echoes bounced off dusty walls,
Like grapes in bowls at raucous balls.
Each corner held a tale to share,
Wrapped in laughter, light as air.

With books upon the shelves so high,
They chuckled softly, 'Give us a try!'
I opened one, it promptly sneezed,
Something tickled, as my funny bone teased.

So off I wandered through the past,
Where every riddle left me aghast.
With smiles tucked in each ancient fold,
I pet the stories, oh so bold.

Treasures Hidden in Plain Sight

Gold is precious, or so they say,
But where do riches hide each day?
I searched my couch, the laundry bin,
And found a quarter, oh what a win!

With breadcrumbs scattered, crumbs of fate,
The cat thinks 'Snacks! Let's celebrate!'
But I just grin, for life's delight,
Is in the search, not the blingy light.

In shoeboxes, under trees,
I found lost treasures, yes, indeed!
A paperclip, a pencil too,
A note that read, 'I love you!'

So next time you feel poor or weak,
Just hunt for giggles, not the peak.
For in the little things we share,
Are diamonds bright beyond compare.

The Simple Heartbeat of Existence

A heartbeat thumps, it's quite a show,
Like drummers tapping, row by row.
With laughter bubbling in between,
We find the fun in every scene.

I danced this morning in my socks,
With cereal crunch, embracing flocks.
The cat just stared with wide-eyed glee,
While plotting schemes of kitty spree.

With oddball moments, life's parade,
Like slipping on a banana's shade.
We laugh at timing, we laugh at fate,
Turn minutes into a funny state.

So if you hear that rhythmic beat,
Join in the dance, get on your feet!
For in each quirk and silly chase,
Is where we find our joyful place.

Reclaiming Lost Moments

In the fridge, my lunch lays still,
Forgotten sandwich, such a thrill.
I find it now, a week or two,
Dried-out bread and moldy hue.

Moments slip beneath the couch,
With dust bunnies, they often crouch.
I reach to grab, oh what a sight,
A long-lost sock, much worse than fright!

Clock ticks fast, but time's a tease,
Next week's plans are such a breeze.
I sneeze and blink, then it's all gone,
Like socks in dryers—poof! Move on.

So here we laugh at mishaps brief,
Each little blunder, a comic relief.
With open arms, we'll take the leap,
To find joy in moments, lost or deep.

Soft Echoes of Life's Lessons

Grandma's wisdom rings so clear,
Yet here I am, still missing beer.
She said, "Don't sweat the silly stuff,"
But tangled wires can feel quite tough.

The lesson learned: don't take a nap,
Unless it's scheduled on the map.
I woke up once surrounded by
A flock of ducks that made me cry.

I thought I'd soar, like a bird in flight,
Instead, I tripped on curtains bright.
Life's elegantly clumsy, so it seems,
Like sticky notes and shattered dreams.

So here's the laugh, let wisdom ring,
With soap in hand, we'll scrub and sing.
A little mess makes life so sweet,
As we chase echoes on our feet.

A Journey through the Ordinary

Every Monday feels like déjà vu,
Pajamas worn, I bid adieu.
With coffee spills and toast that's burnt,
I'll walk this road with lessons learned.

Traffic lights dance in chaotic grace,
As I try to keep up the pace.
GPS says, "You've gone too far!"
I swear my car's a shooting star.

Shopping lists become a game,
"Must-gets" turn into a mental fame.
I seek tomatoes, find laundry soap,
In aisles of chaos, I still hope.

So let the ordinary be my muse,
With every laugh, let's refuse to lose.
For in the mundane, treasures lie,
Just look a bit closer and watch joy fly.

Where Dreams and Reality Converge

My dreams take flight on wings of cheese,
Reality kicks in, "What's your fees?"
I chase the stars on Wednesday night,
While sleep slips in—oh, what a fright!

Reality calls with laundry piles,
One sock missing, unkempt styles.
I question fate with mismatched shoes,
Yet through it all, I'll sing the blues.

Sometimes my thoughts sprout wings of gold,
A fridge full of leftovers, two weeks old.
Yet in the chaos, a dream breaks through,
"Just keep dancing," it whispers, "you."

As dreams and life do twist and twirl,
I'll laugh along as moments unfurl.
In this wacky world, we shall engage,
With joy and giggles, let's turn the page.

The Hum of Everyday Life

In the morning light, I spill my brew,
Caffeine dreams wake, as they often do.
Cats chase shadows, a grand charade,
While I chase lists that never quite fade.

Toasters pop like fireworks, a surprise,
Burnt toast drama with a side of fries.
My sock's on a mission, a great escape,
In this circus of chaos, there's always tape.

Neighbors are busy with their hedge clippers,
While I ponder life with my coffee drippers.
Oh, what a thrill, this wild dance we share,
In every mishap, a love affair.

Laughter erupts at the silliest sight,
Like my cat in a box, what a pure delight!
With each silly moment that steals the show,
We find in the mundane, a joyful flow.

A Voyage through Simple Secrets

A squirrel's grand heist for an acorn treat,
Leaves me in stitches, my heart skips a beat.
As I sail through life in a paper boat,
Laughing at puddles, feeling quite remote.

In my kitchen, I mix chaos and glee,
Flour on the ceiling, where could it be?
With spatula swords, I duel my fate,
As the dinner burns, it's all first-rate!

At the park, I trip over unseen shoes,
Make new friends with a duck, what a ruse!
We share our crumbs, in the golden sun,
Together we giggle, oh what fun!

Life's greatest treasures tucked in each day,
In silly blunders, we laugh and play.
So let's hoist our sails, on this whimsical ride,
With joy as our compass, let's glide outside.

Reawakening the Forgotten Joys

Underneath the bed, where dust bunnies dwell,
I found my lost socks, oh what a tale to tell!
They conspired to vanish, in some grand escape,
While I played detective with my spoon-shaped cape.

The world is a carnival, masks not required,
A slip on a peel leaves us all so inspired.
Like raindrops on rooftops, we dance without care,
Embracing the awkward, with laughter to spare.

Each moment is magic, wrapped in disguise,
Like the time I confused my glasses for fries.
So here's to the cackles, the slips, and the falls,
In the hilarity of life, joy always calls.

Let's bounce like old tunes on a jukebox crack,
With a heart full of giggles, we'll never look back.
For buried in laughter, our treasures lie deep,
In the art of the funny, our spirits will leap.

Beneath the Surface of Tomorrow

In every step we take today,
A sock lost in the dryer may sway.
Tomorrow's plans are made of fluff,
Yet we all act like we're tough.

The coffee spills, the toast gets burned,
And yet the lessons aren't just learned.
A hiccup here, a laugh right there,
Life's just a circus of love and care.

Cats plotting world domination schemes,
While we chase after fanciful dreams.
With maps that lead to places unknown,
We dance through chaos, never alone.

So grab a hat, spin in your chair,
Life's like a dance, without a care.
Wrap it all up with a smile or two,
Tomorrow's waiting—bring your crew!

The Subtle Art of Being

In a world where pants are optional,
And coffee flows like it's intentional.
We try to figure out our place,
With mismatched socks, an awkward grace.

Navigating life with a wink and a grin,
Who knew that laughter could be such a win?
The cat thinks it rules our humble abode,
While we contemplate our life code.

Chasing dreams like they're butterflies,
Stumbling over truths in disguise.
With each little trip, we learn to fall,
The subtle art, oh, it charms us all.

So here we are, in all our glory,
Writing this laughable, messy story.
Life's just a puzzle, we fit piece by piece,
And in this chaos, we find our peace.

Serendipity's Quiet Call

While wandering down a bumpy road,
I tripped on dreams and dropped my load.
A muffin fell, my plans went askew,
And out of chaos, a friendship grew.

In the market of misplaced delight,
The pickles dance like it's Friday night.
A squirrel steals my sandwich with flair,
Leaving me laughing in thin air.

Today's regifted surprises appear,
Like socks that never belong, but cheer.
With pizza poems and coffee spins,
We find the joy hidden beneath our skins.

So embrace the mess, celebrate the fall,
Serendipity rings its quirky call.
With each upside-down twist of fate,
Life's best moments, we just can't wait.

Dancing with Shadows

In the glow of the moon, we twirl and sway,
With shadows that giggle, come out and play.
Our feet tap out the rhythms of life,
While braving the chaos, dancing through strife.

The toaster burns, the cat decides to prance,
And who knew bread could lead to romance?
We shuffle through mishaps, a real magic show,
As laughter becomes the glue we bestow.

With socks that clash and jokes sublime,
We find our groove, transcending time.
Through each misstep, we find our way,
Embracing tomorrow with a silly bouquet.

So let's dance with shadows, join the spree,
For in this twirl, we're all fancy free.
Life's a waltz, just follow the beat,
And don't forget to enjoy the feat!

The Threads that Bind Us

In a world so wide and bright,
We trip on shoelaces, what a sight!
Fumbling through the dance of fate,
Laughing at the mighty weight.

From coffee spills to dodging bees,
We form our bonds with minor wees.
Beneath the chaos, we can see,
Life's simple joys, let's just be free!

We share our meals and socks that mismatch,
Helping hands to stir the batch.
Through silly jokes and playful jives,
It's shared laughter that survives.

So here we are, a quirky crew,
In messy rooms, we make do.
With love and giggles, we ignite,
A tapestry of pure delight.

A Gentle Reminder from Nature

The trees, they chat with leaves so bright,
Whispering secrets in the night.
Squirrels race and birds will sing,
Life's a show, let joy take wing.

Grasshoppers leap with carefree glee,
While frogs croak out their symphony.
Nature reminds, with every quirk,
That joy can often be a perk.

When clouds parade like fluffy sheep,
And rain starts falling down in heaps,
We splash in puddles, dance in glee,
In mud we find our jubilee.

So lift your face, embrace the breeze,
For life's a game, meant to please.
Forget the stress, let laughter flow,
Nature shows us how to glow.

Beneath the Storm's Embrace

In stormy weather, what a steal,
Rain-soaked hair, that's quite the deal!
Umbrellas flipped, a comic scene,
Laughing as we dodge the stream.

Lightning flashes, what a show!
Thunder claps, let's dance, let's go!
The downpour sings a merry tune,
We spin like wild, carefree spoons.

Splashes made with every leap,
The world, it spins, but we don't weep.
With friends around, we brave the dark,
In every storm, we'll leave a mark.

So laugh aloud, don't hide away,
Join in the fun of nature's play.
For in the rain, we weave delight,
Under the storm, we shine so bright.

When Stillness Becomes Clarity

In moments when the world is still,
We ponder life with joyous thrill.
A single cup of tea can spark,
Thoughts like fireflies in the dark.

As quiet sits upon our desk,
We find ourselves, it's quite grotesque.
But through the silence, we can see,
Life's not a race, just let it be.

With wandering minds and playful hearts,
In stillness, we discover arts.
So dance in shadows, seek the light,
In calm we find our bits of bright.

Let laughter echo in the void,
For in stillness, we are buoyed.
Embrace the calm, let it reside,
In quirky peace, we take our stride.

The Art of Quiet Revelations

In a bubble bath, I ponder loud,
Rubber ducks float, making me proud.
Life's answers hide 'neath a sudsy sheen,
Who knew wisdom lived in soap and green?

A cat's lazy yawn brings clarity bright,
As I sip my tea, oh what pure delight!
Biscuit crumbs scattered, I laugh with glee,
Finding joy in crumbs feels like victory!

Throw caution near the wind, take a chance,
Dance in pajamas, don't miss the dance!
Laughter is gold, so shine like a star,
Forget all the paths, just go where you are!

When all else fails, find the nearest snack,
For life's little puzzles, chips never lack.
With snacks in hand, I'll muster the cheer,
Ah, sweet epiphanies — just grab a beer!

Beneath the Surface We Roam

Swimming in socks, what a curious sight,
Finding mermaids who giggle at night.
In the depths of my mind, ideas do flow,
But why is my cat trying to steal my show?

Jellybeans rain down from above,
Life's wacky moments, who can help but love?
With candy in pockets, I stroll with glee,
The true treasure hunts inside you and me!

Skateboards and shoelaces, tangled fair play,
Can't tie my shoes, but I'll dance anyway!
In the crazy whirl, I willingly roam,
Discovering the joy that feels like home.

Take a leap off the couch, no need to fear,
With a pillow for landing, I cheer and veer!
For in these small choices, we find our best,
A squeeze of the joy gives life a sweet zest!

Shadows of Simple Truths

Dancing with shadows that play on the wall,
Whispering secrets, they beckon and call.
Life's simple truths hide in giggles and grins,
With every misstep, that's where it begins!

Caught in a hiccup, I laugh till I cry,
With each little stumble, I'm feeling so spry.
Life winks at you from behind silly masks,
Asking just one thing: can you dare to bask?

Banana peels lurking on tiles, oh dear!
Trip over laughter, let go of your fear.
In playful blunders, we find our own way,
Waltzing through chaos, it's truly ballet!

So grab a kazoo, make some noise and cheer,
Embrace every moment that brings you near.
For laughter and joy are perfect companions,
In this wacky show, we're all the champions!

Epiphanies at Dawn

Waking up yawning, the sun's peeking through,
My coffee's a masterpiece — frothy and new.
As I spill on the table, I chuckle and grin,
Messy revelations are where it begins!

Birds chirping gossip, what tales will they tell?
With dreams in my pockets, I'm under their spell.
A chair's my throne, my thoughts take a flight,
In this rhythmic dance, everything feels right.

Juggling my toast while the cat gives me stares,
Who knew simple mornings could birth such affairs?
Spreading jam thick, I're on a wild spree,
Flavors and follies, dear life, set me free!

As dawn morphs to noon under clouds' gentle drift,
I find shiny wisdom tucked inside every gift.
So raise your glass high, let the laughter not cease,
For each little mishap is a taste of true peace!

The Gift of Unasked Questions

Why do socks always stray,
Missing in the dryer's play?
Sometimes it's best not to know,
Like why your cat steals the show.

Questions roam beneath our lips,
Like why we trip on tiny slips.
Life's absurdity brings us cheer,
Especially when we pretzel your ear.

Just ask the universe, it's wise,
Why chocolate tastes like paradise.
You'll find laughter in the absurd,
Laughing at your neighbor's weird bird.

So let's embrace the goofy quest,
Finding joy in our silly jest.
With unasked questions in our head,
We dance like we've just been led.

Threads that Bind Us All

In a world of tangled strings,
Where odd socks dance, and laughter sings,
We're all connected, twine so dear,
The neighbor's dog, your friend's pet deer.

Through coffee spills and silly pranks,
We roll our eyes, we make our thanks.
Friendship's woven with mismatched socks,
Through all the quirks of life that knocks.

So let's embrace the goofy mess,
Life's punchlines come to bless the stress.
Our threads may tangle, laugh of fear,
Together in laughter, we hold each dear.

Unruly yarn that won't unwind,
Yet in its chaos, love we find.
Through ridiculous moments, both big and small,
In this big weave of life, we're all just a ball.

A Journey Beyond the Known

Pack your bags, let's take a ride,
To a place where pretzels dance with pride.
Maps are useless, that's no joke,
Find joy in the funny stroke.

We'll skip over hills made of cheese,
Chasing after giggles in the breeze.
In realms where logic takes a break,
Laughter's the path we'll undertake.

Flip a pancake in the air,
And don't forget your fuzzy bear.
The journey's not about the goal,
But the wild laughter that makes us whole.

So come and leap on clouds of glee,
Where silly rules are meant to be.
Every misadventure brings delight,
On this ride beyond the normal sight.

Serendipity in Stillness

In quiet moments, surprises bloom,
Like peanut butter on a vacuum broom.
The art of doing nothing well,
Is where the hidden treasures dwell.

A butterfly lands on a sandwich spread,
As thoughts dance wildly in your head.
The beauty lies in the pause so sweet,
Where laughter tiptoes on tiny feet.

Take a break from the daily grind,
And let the randomness unwind.
For life's best gems don't need a race,
They flourish in the silliest space.

So embrace the stillness, let it flow,
In the absurdity, treasures grow.
With every idle moment found,
Laughter whispers all around.

The Beauty of Life's Intricacies

In the fridge, a pickle jar,
Leftovers that could tell a tale,
Each crumb a tiny memoir,
Of dinners where we laughed, not frail.

Spilled coffee on my favorite shirt,
It makes me look quite chic, I swear,
Daily dance of joyful dirt,
Life's mess is quite a work of flair.

Birds chirping in a garden wild,
Chasing shadows with a grin,
Every leaf holds dreams compiled,
In chaos, joy often begins.

Socks that never seem to pair,
A closet full of stories untold,
Life's quirks spark laughter everywhere,
In the mundane, adventure unfolds.

Unspoken Truths of the Heart

A secret stash of candy found,
Hiding in the sock drawer tight,
Each piece a joy that knows no bound,
Like little stars in kitchen light.

Loving the sound of rain drops fall,
Dancing roofs that play a tune,
Heartbeats echo, soft and small,
In puddles, you can find the moon.

When cats roll like they own the street,
Sassy tails and haughty airs,
They've conquered corners, that's their feat,
In their world, we are just stairs.

A wink exchanged with that stranger,
A chuckle under the breath,
In awkwardness lies no danger,
For laughter outlives even death.

Kaleidoscope of Everyday Moments

Coffee dreams and cereal thrills,
The morning sun a friendly nudge,
Every moment, laughter spills,
In the mundane, we find our fudge.

Chasing squirrels in the park,
Their zigzag tales keep us amused,
Like tiny sparks that hit the mark,
Nature's jesters, none confused.

Rainbows painted on the walls,
With crayons that run out of ink,
Artistry in just a few calls,
Life's palette makes us smile and think.

A tangle of wires and dreams,
Life's puzzles hardly ever neat,
In every mess, there's laughter seams,
Each knot a story, bittersweet.

The Joy of Unfolding Simple Pleasures

Uncooked pasta makes a great toy,
Spaghetti sculptures rule the night,
With each twirl, comes purest joy,
Twists and turns, what a sight!

Bubbles floating in the breeze,
Chasing them could bring a smile,
Temporary magic, if you please,
A few seconds of blissful style.

The thrill of pizza from the box,
Who needs plates when you've got cheers?
Each slice, a love that never locks,
In moments, we erase our fears.

Laughter bubbles in the air,
With friends, each moment's a feast,
In life's chaos, we find the fair,
Joy flourishes, to say the least.

The Echoing Song of the Ordinary

In morning light, the toast will burn,
But laughter waits for each little turn.
A sock is lost, where could it go?
The life we lead is one big show.

Chasing dreams with half a shoe,
The dog just rolled in something blue.
Life's odd moments make us grin,
A dance with chaos, let's begin!

With mismatched spoons, we stir our fate,
Spilling coffee, it's never too late.
In simple joys, let's take a look,
For every page turns a quirky book.

So raise a cup, join in the fun,
With silly tales, we've just begun.
The ordinary sings a merry song,
In this mad world, we all belong.

The Gentle Reminder of Being

A cat sits proud, surveying all,
While I trip over a wall.
The laundry's piled, like Mount Everest,
Yet here I stand, feeling blessed.

It's the small things that tickle the soul,
Like finding fries, two days old,
In couch cushions, oh what a find,
Reminders of the good, so unconfined.

Chasing sunsets in mismatched shoes,
Laughing at socks with quirky hues.
Let's dance like no one's watching near,
For in this moment, joy is clear.

So here's to mess, and here's to cheer,
To living loud, devoid of fear.
In this grand play, we all take part,
The gentle reminder lives in the heart.

Exploring the Vastness of Now

With a spoon in hand, I search for treasure,
In a bowl of cereal, pure pleasure.
Time's a trickster, pulls a fast one,
But here we are, still having fun.

A moment's pause, a wink from fate,
A dance of jello on my plate.
In every tick, a chance to cheer,
In this vastness, love is near.

Let's sail on socks across the floor,
In life's great game, we can explore.
With giggles as our guiding star,
It doesn't matter just where we are.

In simple bliss, we find the glow,
As laughter leads, we freely flow.
So grab the now, let's take a bow,
For in this life, we'll make it wow!

Echoes of Past and Present

Oh what a past, with cringes and glee,
That time I wore two shirts, not one, you see!
The fashion trends, so odd and bright,
Now I just grin at the silly sight.

Gather 'round, for stories unfold,
Of spilled drinks and secrets told.
The echoing laugh, a familiar sound,
In this quirky life, joy is found.

Memories dance in a silly jig,
Reminding us to laugh, not dig.
For each mishap writes its own tale,
In every stumble, we shall prevail.

So here's to past and today's embrace,
With goofy smiles, let's set the pace.
In echoes of laughter, we find our way,
Together forever, come what may.

Chronicles of Simple Joys

A warm cup hugs my hands tight,
Coffee spills, but that's alright.
The cat sprawls on the sunny floor,
And snores like he's won a great war.

Each sock lost tells its own tale,
Of laundry adventures and epic fail.
A dance-off with a broom in sight,
Oh, this housework's a pure delight.

Chasing bubbles in the warm breeze,
Laughter echoes among the trees.
A slide down the hill with a shout,
Who knew joy could be this profound?

With sprinkles on cupcakes we cheer,
Wandering in our garden of fear.
Living each day like it's a game,
It's the quirks that keep life insane!

Beneath the Veil of Ordinary

The world spins, wrapped in routine,
Yet chaos lurks where things get clean.
A lost car key found in the fridge,
Life's oddities dance on a ridge.

Neighbors argue over a fence,
Rabbits plotting their escape hence.
The mailman hums a silly tune,
While I search for my lost shoe's boon.

Pancakes burn, but laughter ignites,
We gather 'round for silly fights.
Each mishap leads to greater tales,
Life's comical dance never pales.

In mundane moments, joy is found,
Like socks that disappear without sound.
So grab a spoon, let's stir the pot,
For the foolish fun is never forgot!

A Symphony of Small Things

A sneeze erupts, then giggles flow,
Bubbles rise in the washing bowl.
A bird who thinks it's Elvis sings,
As we trample on dreams like springs.

The toast pops up with a loud cheer,
Burnt edges? Never fear, my dear!
Spilling cereal leads to a race,
As milk flies all over the place.

The dog wears my hat just to tease,
And wags his tail like he's got keys.
A garden gnome sharing a grin,
Promising mischief about to begin.

In this orchestra of the mundane,
Each note played is sweetly insane.
So dance in your kitchen, give it a whirl,
For small things make the joy unfurl!

Fleeting Glimpses of Truth

A picnic turned into a quest,
With ants that invite themselves as guests.
A spilled drink made for a new design,
In nature's art, we all align.

The ice cream cone takes a swift dive,
A race against time, can we survive?
Laughter erupts with every drip,
Sweet sticky moments on a whim.

A squirrel steals our sandwich with glee,
While birds chirp like they're on a spree.
Sidewalk chalk, a rainbow parade,
Life's hidden gems always displayed.

Between the laughter and silly fights,
There's magic in ordinary sights.
So uncork joy in the most absurd,
For life is poetry, haven't you heard?

Unseen Guidance Along the Way

Just when you think you know the plan,
A squirrel steals your sandwich, oh man.
Life swirls in chaos, a jumbled dance,
Yet, somehow we laugh, given half a chance.

With advice from a pigeon that won't go away,
We follow its strut, ignoring dismay.
In the park, we chat with a tree, quite wise,
Though its answers are mostly just leaves and sighs.

Every twist and turn keeps us on our toes,
Like lost in a maze where nobody knows.
Yet smiles and giggles add flavor to gloom,
While the universe snickers, we still make room.

So raise your glass to the wacky design,
Embrace every hiccup, let chaos align.
Through the mishaps and laughter, we find our way,
With unseen guidance lighting every day.

Life's Quests Without a Map.

They say maps are for fools and scholars alike,
But here I roam, without GPS or bike.
Each step is a riddle, a puzzle to crack,
With my only companion, a snack in my pack.

I sought hidden treasures, most were just crumbs,
My journey's a circus, filled with odd chums.
A talking dog taught me to chase my own tail,
While an umbrella warned me of rain's big fail.

In the quest for wisdom, I found silly tales,
Like how to wear socks that go with fish scales.
There's joy in the wander, a spark in the roam,
For laughter is currency wherever you comb.

So let's toss out the map and dance in the dark,
We'll embrace the absurd, let it leave its mark.
For every mishap, there's fun to be had,
In this life, with its chaos, who could be sad?

Whispers of Existence

Amidst the noise, a soft voice calls,
It giggles and whispers, as irony falls.
When things get too serious, just look around,
Life's silly antics are where laughs are found.

A butterfly trips over its own wings,
As the universe chuckles, so many things.
With each little mishap, a chuckle ensues,
Showing us laughter's the best type of muse.

In gardens of chaos where puppies play chase,
And cats plot their mischief with elegant grace.
There's wisdom in whimsy, a truth we can find,
In the giggles and stumbles that fill up our mind.

So listen for laughter in whispers of fate,
Embrace the delightful, don't hesitate.
For existence is coy, with a wink and a grin,
Eureka! The joy is where life begins.

Unraveling the Unseen Threads

In a world where socks go missing and roam,
We ponder the patterns of destiny's foam.
With threads of mishap intertwined in our fate,
We laugh at the wreckage and celebrate late.

A cat's philosophical debate with a shoe,
Leaves us pondering meanings we never quite knew.
As bananas slip by in outrageous slapstick,
We learn that existence has quite the comic flick.

With yarn tangled up like our thoughts on a day,
We find wisdom in weaves that seem lost on the way.
So grab an old sweater, embrace the dull hue,
Life's patches and seams create something new.

Through laughter and folly, the fabric reveals,
That joy is the stitch that our heart truly feels.
In unraveling moments, we'll find worth in play,
In the grand tapestry, let the silliness stay.

When Silence Speaks Louder

In a room full of chatter, I sit so still,
Listening to whispers, it gives me a thrill.
My friends think I'm quiet, a wallflower, it's true,
But I'm just the DJ of the silent debut.

I see people go on, with stories to tell,
How boring is that? I wish them all well.
Their laughter rings out, but inside I just grin,
For the best punchline's the one you don't spin.

When awkwardness settles, like dust on the shelf,
I think it's quite funny, just being myself.
So let others spill secrets, while I sip my tea,
In the stillness of silence, there's humor for me.

The unspoken moments, oh how they bring glee,
Like soap in the bathtub, so slippery, see?
So next time you talk, be mindful and sly,
For silence might just be the best kind of high.

Tapestry of Unraveled Dreams

Woven threads of wishes, all tangled and bright,
A tapestry hanging, revealing delight.
Each knot tells a tale, of hopes that once bloomed,
But ended up twisted, now slightly marooned.

My dreams like a laundry line, flapping in the breeze,
Get caught in the branches, oh, what a tease!
I planned for the future, a smooth, straight road,
But ended up on a rollercoaster of code.

From riches to rags, in a blink of an eye,
I thought I was soaring, but now I'm just shy.
So I chuckle and weave, with a wink and a grin,
For reality and dreams, it's a tangled-up win!

So here's to the dreams, all ragged and worn,
They're the best kind of art, just waiting to be born.
In this tapestry life, with colors we find,
Laughter's the glue that keeps us aligned.

The Serene Poetry of Today

Today is a canvas, simple and sweet,
With splashes of chaos, a delightful treat.
I wake up and stumble, my coffee's gone cold,
Yet there's beauty in messes, truths waiting to unfold.

The cat claims my lap, it's a throne made of fur,
While socks without partners dance, oh what a stir!
I scribble my verses, with left and with right,
And chuckle at life, as it tickles my sight.

In the quiet of moments, like butter on toast,
I find silly stories that I love the most.
The mundane can sparkle, if you look with delight,
For each day's an adventure, a whimsical flight.

So raise up your glasses, to laughter, not gloom,
In this beautiful chaos, let joy brightly bloom.
With a wink and a nod, let's dance through the fray,
For the poetry of now makes a glorious display!

Dancing with Time's Fickle Partner

Time waltzes around, in a dress made of gold,
But my two left feet have me feeling quite bold.
I trip and I stumble on seconds and ticks,
While the clock just chuckles, like it knows all the tricks.

It spins me in circles, on moments I chase,
And just when I'm ready, it quickens the pace.
Like a partner who teases, and then steps away,
Time's got its own plans, it's a rollercoaster play.

With calendars flashing, and deadlines that loom,
I dance with my worries, as they all seem to bloom.
Yet I giggle and twirl, as I remember the fun,
For life is a party, and I'm never quite done.

So let's boogie with minutes, let's tango with hours,
Amidst all the chaos, let's savor the flowers.
With laughter and joy, I'll twirl till I drop,
For the more that I dance, the more I won't stop!

A Personal Map of Wonder

I searched for the treasure, but found my shoe,
A map made of ketchup, my guide was a goo.
The X marked the spot, on my neighbor's lawn,
With a shovel in hand, at the break of dawn.

The compass spun wildly, it seemed out of style,
I followed a squirrel, it led me a mile.
In the end, I found giggles, not gold or more,
A treasure of laughter, who could ask for more?

Pirate hats on, with kitchen forks raised,
We conquered the world, in our backyard glazed.
A world made of wonder, no maps to unfold,
In each goofy moment, life's riches are gold.

So if you are lost, with no treasure in sight,
Just dance with your worries, make laughter your light.
For the real adventure, it's all in the fun,
Who knew that life's riches were all just a pun?

The Hidden Dance of Time

Time wears a tutu, it twirls and it spins,
It tickles the seconds, and giggles within.
I tried to take notes, but my pen ran away,
Time rapped on my door, "Let's party and play!"

With clocks as my partners, we danced through the day,
In moments so silly, I'd forget what to say.
Each tick-tock a wink, each tock-tock a cheer,
We clapped and we spun, with no hint of fear.

When I tripped over minutes, time chuckled with glee,
"Don't worry my friend, just be as goofy as me!"
As shadows grew long, and day turned to night,
We swayed with the moon, in a dazzling light.

So if you find time, trying to run away,
Just dance with the moment, let whimsy hold sway.
For in life's waltz, between laughs and the chime,
We find all the rhythm, in the hidden dance of time.

Embracing Life's Unwritten Pages

With pencils unsharpened, I started to write,
On pages unwritten, with crayons so bright.
Each scribble a promise, each doodle a dream,
Life's book is a canvas—oh what a theme!

The bird on page three ate my homework with flair,
A dragon in purple popped out from the air.
Every blank space, an adventure unknown,
With rainbows and jellybeans, the more I had grown.

I spilled all my dreams, in a splash of pure fun,
With stickers and glitter, I danced in the sun.
So many blank chapters, let's write them with cheer,
With giggles and whimsy, each moment is here!

So grab all your colors, don't fret and don't pout,
Embrace every page, let the laughter break out.
For life's just a story, and the pen's in your hand,
In the wild ocean of joy, let your heart be the land.

Journey through a Whispered Path

I took a short stroll down a path made of giggles,
With bushes of candy and trees that do wiggles.
Each step that I took, brought a tickle to toes,
As butterflies whispered, "Here anything goes!"

A rabbit with glasses, he offered me tea,
With biscuits of marshmallow, as sweet as can be.
We skipped past the puddles of laughter and cheer,
With clouds shaped like puppies, spreading gladness near.

The wicked old gnome tried to steal all my snacks,
But we danced in a circle, he quickly backtracked.
We twirled with the daisies, we laughed at the sun,
For on this wild journey, each moment's pure fun.

So if you feel lost on life's winding pathway,
Just follow the whispers, and chuckle away.
In the journey of joy, with a heart full of mirth,
You'll find the best treasures are right here on Earth.

www.ingramcontent.com/pod-product-compliance
Lightning Source LLC
Chambersburg PA
CBHW051701160426
43209CB00004B/981